AF207749

The Handmaiden Conspiracy
Study Guide

The Handmaidens Conspiracy STUDY GUIDE

by Donna Howell, Professor Rob Weddle
Defender Publishing Crane, MO 65633

© 2024 Defender Publishing
All Rights Reserved. Published 2024

ISBN: 978-1-948014-86-1

Printed in the United States of America.

A CIP catalog record of this book is available from the Library of Congress.

Cover design by Justen Faull, Jeffrey Mardis
Interior design by Katherine Lloyd

CONTENTS

REFLECTION QUESTIONS

INTRODUCTION

Welcome to the study guide for *The Handmaiden Conspiracy*, a biblical study book by author Donna Howell, addressing the issues of women in leadership, pastoral, evangelical, and missionary positions within the church. From the SkyWatch TV summary to her book, we read the central goals of this work, along with the chief points of enrichment for the Body of Christ as a whole:

The veil was not the only thing that Christ's arrival on earth tore asunder. Social and religious barriers, serving to draw lines between specific people groups for thousands of years before His arrival, were suddenly in light of His Great Commission transformed. Never would a tax collector, a zealot, and a traditional Jew share a meal together in peace...but following just a short time in Jesus presence, these barriers crumbled. The influence that Christ had on the men in His day has been celebrated for two thousand years. The overlooked question within mainstream Christianity remains to be: What influence did He have upon women, and what statements did His words and actions make in relation to gender equality? Is it possible that while Jesus Christ, Himself, recognized appropriate gender roles, He also intentionally began the first Women's Liberation Movement? As sensational as this may sound, the proof is in the Word of God, and in the proper contextual analysis of it.

In *The Handmaiden Conspiracy*, you will:

1) Follow the cultural and historic backdrop behind Paul's words in 1 Corinthians and 1 Timothy—the trouble verses in relation to the issue of women leadership in the Church and understand more properly what he was responding to when the epistles were written;

2) Observe the Principal of Internal Consistency at play throughout repeated accounts of Scripture openly describing women preaching, teaching, prophesying, and leading with powerful voices in the Body of Christ and Saint Peter's acknowledgment that this very activity, foretold in Joel 2:28, began on the Day of Pentecost;

3) Discover what the original Greek nouns and adjectives meant in Paul's greeting orders, the women that he was both commissioning and commending as fellow ministers of his own circle (Phoebe, Priscilla, Junia, and several others who were suddenly equal to men in ministerial commission), and the misleading translational and interpretational errors that continuously assist in perpetuating an erroneous concept that women should always remain silent in the work of Christ.

4) Reflect upon the women Jesus knew, both from Scripture as well as in person, and the groundbreaking, permanent changes He made regarding their rights, their value, and their role in delivering His message to the world;

5) Revisit and refine some ancient, yet inaccurate, ideas the Body of Christ has had regarding the Bible s most talked-about women, such as Eve, Mary (the mother of Christ), Mary Magdalene, Judge Deborah, Prophetess Huldah, and others;

6) Understand why the prohibition of women as equals in leadership is not only unbiblical, it is actually doing harm to the Church today.

HOW TO USE
THIS STUDY GUIDE

This study guide is designed for group or individual study, although, like any "deep theological dive," you will more than likely get more out of it in a group setting. In each chapter, you'll read a chapter summary and the main points, followed by a set of questions for that chapter. In these questions you'll find a variety of formats, including multiple-choice, true and false, fill-in-the-blank, and short answer.

As you finish reading a chapter, you are encouraged to work through the questions for that chapter in the study guide. Page numbers matching the print edition of the book are given for most questions, not so you'll skip the reading, but rather, to help you more quickly locate the answer.

Additionally, in the last section of the guide you'll find a "reflection question" for each chapter. Again, these can be completed in individual study, but are ideal for a group setting.

Whether you study on your own or with a group, our prayer is that this guide helps you gain more understanding of this hot-button topic.

Chapter 1

THE CULTURAL INTERPRETATION DEBATE

CHAPTER 1 SUMMARY:

Chapter 1 opens by conveying the story of author Donna Howell's very successful appearance on *The Jim Bakker Show*, followed closely by extreme negativism on the part of those commenters online who believed she was preaching the so-called "fallacy" of the legitimacy of women occupying ministerial positions. The author explains that *The Handmaiden's Conspiracy* was NOT written with a radical feminist agenda, in an attempt to "prove" women are the same as men, or that women can do anything men can do. She states we must all embrace our differences. She goes on to explain that this book was not written in the spirit of "payback" to her detractors, but rather, to explain that *all Scripture* must be studied in the original languages (Greek and Hebrew), when it appears to be establishing a rule about how we are to live today, *especially* when the English translations so familiar to our culture never truly captured the true meanings of the original words in the first place, which is the case here. The primary thrust of this chapter is to keep the following in mind concerning every verse in the Bible: the genre, the author, the audience, the circumstances, the cultural climate and language behind the verse, and the surrounding text.

MAIN POINTS:

- Author Donna Howell's central message is to embolden members of the Church Body to rise up and take ownership of their role in the Great Commission, with passion and love for all
- If any plan is carried out by man, it will fail; but if it is of God, nobody will be able to overthrow it

- The primary issue of the book is whether or not a woman is truly in God's will by being a minister
- We cannot pick and choose what we want to believe from Scripture and ignore (or improperly apply) the rest; so if there are verses allowing for women ministers at the time of Paul (and there are ample examples of this in the Greek, as the student will discover early on in this class), we must only apply prohibitions when the circumstances are the same or similar to those Paul was reacting to in the "prohibition verses"
- Regarding the differences between men and women, we should continue perpetuating the goal of equality precisely because of how we are *different*, not in the interest of proving we're the *same*
- Incorrect application of Scripture results in erroneous interpretation and vice versa
- The injury of misinformation spreads distortion like a brushfire
- The two most important deductions any reader of the Bible should be making are these: 1) What God was communicating to His original audience through the human writer at the time it was written? and 2) What normative regulations for daily life does that present for us today?
- For proper biblical interpretation, we must consider the genre, author, audience, circumstances, cultural language behind the verse, and surrounding text

QUESTIONS:

1. (Page 8) Donna's appearance on *The Jim Bakker Show* was a huge success. The author herself admits her words were nothing new, but apparently the church is so _____ for _____ that it only takes one voice to say the simplest thing.

2. (Pages 8–10) The people whom the author refers to as "Internet trolls" were attacking her because:
    A. They were under the conviction of the Holy Spirit
    B. They didn't agree with her theology
    C. She is a woman
    D. She spoke too loud

3. (Page 10) Summarize what Donna means by "Gamaliel logic."

4. TRUE OR FALSE: On page 16, the author states that many in today's culture cherry pick Bible verses that suit them, accepting the "cultural issue" argument when it's convenient and dismissing it when it isn't.

5. Considering the text on page 16, is the author coming from a *radical feminist* point of view? Why or why not?

6. TRUE OR FALSE: On page 17, Donna states that, often, "berating" responses to women ministers come from men [and sometimes other women] who are in leadership.

7. According to page 17, explain what the author means when she says, "Feminism has…caused extreme harm to the concept of equality."

8. On page 17, Donna states, "The justice that modern feminism fights for results in _____ _____ and _____ _____ for those in the fight."

9. What is the author's meaning on page 18 when she says, "the Bible can be a dangerous tool"?

10. On page 22, in the story of Sarah, Jenny and Amanda, Donna states, "Jenny acknowledges that her words were _____ correctly, but the _____ of them was distorted, and they therefore conveyed an erroneous meaning."

11. On page 25, according to *Barnes,* "the evil here" is preachers who stand from a pulpit and speak for God without "_____ _____," due in part to a lack of understanding the _____ at the time the book was written.

12. What does the author mean on page 27 when she says we must understand the "voice" behind the text?

13. As per the author's text on page 29, why don't some people want to hear the truth?

14. According to pages 30–32, what is the relevance of a "holy kiss," the sacrifice of animals on the altar, and Paul's instruction to Timothy to drink a little wine for his stomach problems (1 Timothy 5:23)?

    A. We have to consider what God was communicating to His original audience through the human writer at the time.

B. We must keep in mind the normal/normative guidelines for daily life the Scriptures present for us today.

C. Both A and B

D. Neither A nor B

15. TRUE OR FALSE: As per page 38, "the most accurate translation" of the Bible is not *necessarily* the King James Version, but the original manuscripts, written by the original authors, in the original languages, as God first delivered it to humanity—all English versions have involved human interpretation (and therefore possibly involve errors) in the translation process.

Chapter 2

INTERNAL CONSISTENCY

CHAPTER 2 SUMMARY:

Author Donna Howell begins by asking: If one takes a literal interpretation of 1 Corinthians 14:34–35 and 1 Timothy 2:11–12, what *can* women do in church? Can they speak at all? Preach? Sing? Then she states, "But if what we're talking about truly is a matter of *correct* interpretation, then these questions wouldn't be necessary in the first place, because the circumstances Paul was addressing have nothing to do with these issues." Donna outlines the internal consistency of Scriptures unrelated to the "prohibition passages" that *endorse* women leaders, teachers and ministers, including a list of women in the ministry in Paul's time (one of whom may have been a pastor or high leader over him earlier on).

MAIN POINTS:
- There is glaring evidence that Paul actually *supported* women having roles in Church leadership
- We know, first of all, that women were present in the Upper Room on the Day of Pentecost, which is documented in Acts 2:1–6; these women were among the men who ran out into the streets preaching the Gospel that same day when thousands of souls were saved as a result
- The New Testament Church met in the homes of believers, and examples of female leaders in these "home churches" were John Mark's mother Mary in Jerusalem (Acts 12:12); Lydia in Philippi (Acts 16:14–15); Priscilla (alongside her husband Aquila) in Ephesus and Rome (Acts 18:19, 26; 1 Corinthians 16:19; Romans 16:3–5); Phoebe in Cenchrea (Romans 16:1); and Apphia in Colossae (Philemon 2)

- Acts 2:18 says the "women" or "handmaidens" shall prophecy (a word meaning "to *teach*, refute, reprove, admonish"), which was a fulfillment of an ancient prophecy from Joel
- When Paul mentions Phoebe in Romans 16, he was probably referring to a woman in a position of pastoral leadership over a congregation
- Romans 16:2, using the Greek word *prostatis* ("overseer"), indicates that Phoebe might have been a pastoral figure to Paul in the past
- In Romans 16:7, Paul writes, "Salute Andronicus and Junia, my kinsmen, and my fellow-prisoners, who are of note among the apostles, who also were in Christ before me"; "Junia" (Greek literal: *Junian*) is feminine, while the Greek word *en* (translated in English as "among") indicates she was an apostle alongside the men, as the scholars, theologians, language experts, historians, and Church Fathers cited in this book have taught since Paul's day
- Galatians 3:28 says, "There is neither Jew nor Greek, there is neither bond nor free, there is *neither male nor female*: for *ye are all one* in Christ Jesus"
- Paul did not attempt to place any kind of spiritual "off switch" upon the giftings of the Holy Spirit in relation to women; Paul respected the Word of God as it relates to women preaching, teaching, and prophesying as the women did on the Day of Pentecost under the guidance of the Spirit: Equality of all *in Christ*

QUESTIONS:

1. What are some of the questions that arise when we use a literal and extreme interpretation of Paul's words about women speaking and preaching in church in *all* times and cultures?
2. Acts 2 states that women were called to "prophesy," the Greek word being *propheteuo,* which means to:
    - A. teach
    - B. refute and reprove
    - C. admonish (correct or reprimand)
    - D. comfort others
    - E. all of the above

3. According to page 49, the Greek word *propheteuo* in Acts 2:17–18 does not mean "a ____ for God," but a ____ ____ for God's holy nation (God's people).

4. TRUE OR FALSE (page 53): A better way to express the last half of David's Psalm 28:11, "The Lord gave the word: *great was the company of those that published it*," would be "great was the group of women who proclaimed (the Word of the Lord)."

5. (Page 56) In Acts 18:24–26, *both* Priscilla and Aquila ____ the Jewish scholar Apollos:
    A. chastised
    B. corrected
    C. cooked for
    D. none of the above

6. Many scholars believe that Paul introduced Priscilla *before* Aquila in Romans 16:3 because (page 57):
    A. He was being chivalrous
    B. This was customary at the time
    C. He didn't actually do this; some believe this was a mistranslation
    D. Priscilla was more "active" as a teacher and leader in their home church

7. TRUE OR FALSE (page 58): In Romans 16:3, when referring to Priscilla, Paul used the ancient Greek word *synergos*, which means "servant."

8. TRUE OR FALSE (pages 60–61): In Romans 16:21, Paul uses the same Greek word, *synergos*, or "workfellow," to describe Timothy, one of Paul's most trusted and beloved pastors/preachers/teachers, as he did Priscilla, meaning she was at least equivalent in ministerial function to Timothy.

9. Who were the two female "fellowlabourers" Paul mentions in Philippians 4:2–3 (page 61)?

10. According to the author on page 65, the word "succourer" in Romans 16:2 is drawn from the Greek *prostatis*. In breaking down the meaning, the author states that *prostatis* means:

    A. to stand before others

    B. to stand "over" others (similar to an "overseer")

    C. church leader

    D. all of the above

11. On page 73, according to the author, Junia didn't fear persecution or imprisonment, but rather, _____ it.

12. TRUE OR FALSE: In Galatians 3:28, Paul's foremost goal was to discuss women's rights in church clergy (page 75).

13. TRUE OR FALSE: On pages 78–79, Donna states that, while Paul saw us all "as one," this didn't necessarily apply to women being leaders in the church.

Chapter 3

CONTEXT OF 1 CORINTHIANS (PART ONE)

CHAPTER 3 (PART ONE) SUMMARY:

When the proper tools are not utilized for interpreting Scripture, misunderstandings and misinterpretations abound. Author Donna Howell walks us through the steps in discovering the true meaning of a Bible verse. This is followed by a lengthy description of the city of Corinth at the time Paul wrote his first letter to the church in that mighty city, and begins to unravel why Paul had statements that, on the surface, appear to forbid women to teach, preach or even *speak* in church. Then we find out what temple prostitutes, braids, and gold all have in common and what they imply in regard to the prohibition of women speaking out in service.

MAIN POINTS:

- Three steps to properly interpreting the meaning of any Bible verse: 1) The original circumstances must be determined; 2) Similar (or exact) circumstances of today must be determined; 3) The "relative" instructions apply to today's reader after a fair comparison of the two preceding factors have been determined, and in a way that preserves the spirit of the principles taught.
- The *hetairai*, or temple prostitutes, of Corinth were richly dressed, articulate, heavily painted, schooled in oratory skills and rhetoric, and every hair was in the right place as they flitted about society and "owned" every room they entered. They were not worshiped as gods, themselves—and as women, they were certainly marginalized in society in comparison to men—but their bodies were the conduit

through which the pagan gods were worshiped and honored. They were often welcome to share their thoughts and opinions regarding spirituality or theology, *especially* in the presence of men who believed them to communicate the will of the gods (like oracles)

- Corinthian believers were engaging in sexual perversion left and right. They were taking each other to court and allowing pagans to make legal rulings upon matters that were spiritual in nature. Immoral conduct was warping the sacred communion observances. Doctrinal errors were rampant. The believers were tripping over themselves to prove that "their way" was the best way for their church and that "their theology" was correct; this escalated to the point that feuds and disruption during services were commonplace, plummeting each gathering into chaos

- The church in Corinth was in a constant state of commotion. People were saying the equivalent to, "My theology is more accurate than yours, because I follow" a certain person.

- "Sacred prostitution" was influencing the entire city, and sexual perversion was common, including incest.

- Paul supported witnesses of the Gospel representing themselves agreeably to one audience in one way and another way to a different audience as it pertains to the social and cultural demands/expectations

- By Paul discussing the proper way a woman should "pray" and "prophesy" while her head is covered *in church* (11:5), he is openly acknowledging that women are allowed to speak in church

QUESTIONS:

1. According to the author (pages 83–84), to properly interpret a Bible verse, we have to separate the _____ from the _____, in addition to nailing down what is _____.

2. List some examples of how Paul persecuted the Church before becoming a follower of "The Way" (page 84–85).

3. To better understand 1 Corinthians 14:34–35, what type of city was Corinth (page 86)?

4. According to page 88, Corinth was a "cesspool of religious prostitution." Its sexual perversion was so severe that, in surrounding

regions, any woman known for her loose behavior was referred to as a "_____ _____."

5. TRUE OR FALSE: On page 88, the author states that Corinth believers were influenced by "pagan convictions and mystery cults."

6. What was Paul's chief concern in his letter to the Corinthians (page 88–89)?
    A. Their beliefs on the second coming of Jesus were skewed
    B. He wanted to straighten out their thinking on baptism
    C. Explanations on the true meaning of being a disciple of Jesus
    D. Their loyalties were divided

7. According to page 90, what word best describes Corinthian Christians at the time Paul wrote his letter to them?
    A. Divided
    B. United
    C. Passive
    D. Devoted

8. According to the author in chapter three, which issue(s) did Paul address in his letter to the church in Corinth?
    A. Prostitution
    B. Dissension/division
    C. Incest
    D. Christians taking each other to court
    E. All of the above

9. On page 92, the author lists which two factors as being "unquestionably connected" in the Corinthian church?
    A. Pros and cons of being married; prostitution
    B. Erroneous theology; pride
    C. Sexual immorality; dissension
    D. Food offered to idols; servantship

10. On page 95, the author lists two attributes that must be sustained if people are ever to be won to Christ: _____ and _____.

11. TRUE OR FALSE: The author states on page 97 that it's ok to "storm the doors of a church with vigorous proselytizing" if it wins some to Jesus.

Chapter 3

CONTEXT OF 1 CORINTHIANS
(PART TWO)

CHAPTER 3 (PART TWO) SUMMARY:

Carrying on in chapter three of author Donna Howell's fascinating study on women in leadership and ministry in the church, she continues to discuss the church in Corinth, including the chaos it housed. She digs deeper into the Corinthian culture, involving things like temple goddesses and prostitutes, and how they held higher social positions than women in other cultures. Rather than making snap judgments for Bible verses we *think* we understand, she presents a wealth of research which points to the true meaning behind some of Paul's words, encouraging us to do the same when it comes to controversial and/or confusing Scriptures.

MAIN POINTS:

- When Paul speaks of "man" in certain key verses, he's referring to "mankind"
- The entire letter of 1 Corinthians was addressing *chaos in the church*. So, statements like "women should keep silence" must be taken alongside others such as "God is not the author of confusion" and "Let all things be done decently and in order"
- The women in Corinth were talking during service, which is why Paul told them not to "keep talking"
- Examples of women serving in leadership positions in the New Testament church include: John Mark's mother Mary in Jerusalem (Acts 12:12); Lydia in Philippi (Acts 16:14–15); Priscilla (alongside her husband Aquila) in Ephesus and Rome (Acts: 18:19, 26; 1

Corinthians 16:19; Romans 16:3–5); Phoebe in Cenchrea (Romans 16:1); and Apphia in Colossae (Philemon 2).

- Paul was silencing women because of the pagan women who didn't know their place in the Church of Jesus Christ
- Our best bet for interpretation is to see what is on the page, look into the backdrop, understand all contributing factors and circumstances, and *then* apply the regulations to similar or exact circumstances today
- Paul never said in 1 Corinthians 14 that women are not permitted to be preachers or teachers of the Word. Paul was silencing the disruption

QUESTIONS:

1. FINISH THIS SENTENCE FROM PAGE 98: "(In Corinth at the time) For a woman to go into a place of worship and pray or prophesy with her head uncovered was to…"

2. TRUE OR FALSE: On page 99 the author states that, as per 1 Corinthians 12:6, when Paul stated that "there are diversities of operations, but it is the same God which worketh all in all," the "all" in this case is referring to "both men and women"

3. SHORT ANSWER: As per the author on page 101, why is it so important to view the Great Commission as an all-inclusive endeavor?

4. Considering our subject matter, why does the author go into an explanation of "chaos" on pages 103–104, and *when* to speak in tongues in chapter three, when it doesn't appear to be relevant at first?
    A. She admits she is "chasing rabbits," going off on an unrelated tangent
    B. Following these verses in 1 Corinthians 14 we find the infamous passage about women keeping silent in churches
    C. Because the gift of tongues is for both men and women
    D. None of these answers apply

5. FILL-IN-THE-BLANK: Even though Paul had over 30 different Greek words for "talk" to choose from, in 1 Corinthians 14:34,

when he said, "for it is not permitted unto them [women] to speak," the word for "speak" here is the Greek *laleo*, which simply means "to _____," but is actually better translated as "to keep on _____" (page 109).

6. SHORT ANSWER: According to page 110, why were Christian women in Corinth "especially chatty," as per the author?

7. On page 111, the author says, "Paul never placed gender _____ upon Holy Spirit gifts, which without a doubt includes public expounding (teaching, preaching, etc.):

    A. specifics

    B. roles

    C. discrimination

    D. restrictions

8. The author states on page 112 that, according to one theory (herein shown to be flawed), the letter to Corinth was "silencing *all* women" because of...

    A. Their need to submit to their husbands

    B. Morality restrictions

    C. Pagan outbursts

    D. The customs at the time

9. Explain how the "call-and-response theory" may shed light on Paul's true meaning of women keeping silent in church, according to the author on page 113.

Chapter 4

CONTEXT OF 1 TIMOTHY (PART ONE)

CHAPTER 4 (PART ONE) SUMMARY:

Timothy, pastor of the newly planted church in Ephesus, was Paul's "son in the faith" (1 Timothy 1:2). Ephesians contains some of Paul's *seemingly* harshest words against women leaders and speakers in the church, and it is this fascinating study which author Donna Howell embarks on in chapter four. At the time Paul wrote his letters to Timothy, Ephesus was not only one of the wealthiest cities in the area, but one of the most sexually deviant. To understand why Paul said what he did about women in church (and in ministry), it's important we carefully examine the Ephesian culture.

MAIN POINTS:

- Timothy was the pastor of the church in Ephesus that Paul had launched during his second missionary journey
- Ephesus was one of the wealthiest cities in the Mediterranean world, with major trade ports and dealing heavily in the industry of idol-making
- Alongside Minerva and Vesta, Artemis/Diana was considered one of the three "main" goddesses of mythology, and worshipped by many in this area at the time
- Women were revered as professors, sculptors, painters, musicians, and philosophers, among many other illustrious offices. Ephesus was also afflicted with unrestrained sexual worship
- In Paul's day, it wasn't at all abnormal for a person to cherry pick what he or she liked to hear from several religions and mesh them

together in one amalgamated mess of a personal theology (a practice called "syncretism")

- The priestesses of Artemis/Diana saw themselves as the divine mediators between gods and men, and they were revered as such by the males in and around the city
- Ephesus contained an "insane pagan-Christianity unification" (the worst kind of syncretism)

QUESTIONS:

1. SHORT ANSWER: According to the author (page 119–120), what are some of the attributes of Artemis/Diana, whom the people of Ephesus (where Timothy served as pastor to a New Testament Christian church) worshipped?

2. TRUE OR FALSE: Even though many in Ephesus worshipped Artemis/Diana, women were still not considered equal to men in social rights and privileges from many angles (including religious settings, page 120).

3. Donna says on page 121 that Ephesus was "afflicted with unrestrained _____ _____."

4. On page 121, she relays that Acts 19:23–29, 20:1 documents a tumultuous few hours when the entire city was thrown into chaos and many voices in one accord decreed, "Great is Diana of the Ephesians!" What started this uprising?

5. What concept of the new "Christ religion" would the women of Ephesus have already been familiar with, according to the author on page 121?

6. TRUE OR FALSE: On page 122, Donna says that once many people in Ephesus accepted Christ as their savior, they completely turned their back on their former religion(s).

7. SHORT ANSWER: On page 127, Donna relays that, in 1 Timothy, Paul's concerns were not with women wearing braids, pearls, gold, or expensive clothes. What were his concerns?

8. The author states on page 127 that women weaving gold into their braids was the same practice as what group of people?
    A. Wives
    B. Prostitutes
    C. Unmarried women
    D. Women with children

9. TRUE OR FALSE: On page 130, Donna says that 1 Timothy 2:9–10, regarding braids and gold in a woman's hair, *is* a cultural issue, whereas 1 Timothy 2:11–12, "I suffer not a woman to teach, nor to usurp authority over the man," is an absolute regulation.

10. Name the couple who led the church in Ephesus after Paul established it, with the wife being their archetypal "pastor" prior to Timothy (page 130).
    A. Abigail and Nabal
    B. Ruth and Boaz
    C. Ananias and Sapphira
    D. Priscilla and Aquila

11. FILL-IN-THE-BLANK: On page 131, Donna boldly proclaims that "The prohibition against women teachers was a '_____ issue'."

12. FILL-IN-THE-BLANK From 1 Timothy 2:1 through 3:13, the author says Paul was calling Timothy to establish _____ within the church (page 133).

Chapter 4

CONTEXT OF 1 TIMOTHY
(PART TWO)

CHAPTER 4 (PART TWO) SUMMARY:

Continuing author Donna Howell's riveting study on Ephesus, she explains that we must understand the cultural circumstances behind why Paul said what he did to Timothy. Gaining a thorough, "behind-the-scenes" understanding of the paganism and sexual deviancy of the once-great city of Ephesus is *crucial* to discovering the truth behind a set of Bible verses that have caused great division in the church for two millennia.

MAIN POINTS:

- In writing to Timothy, the pastor of the church at Ephesus, there were isolated circumstances that applied to the culture at the time, and it was those very circumstances Paul had to address in his letters

- Sex magic, mystery cults, pagan idolatry, prostitution, and women as mediators and oracles between God (or gods) and man were infiltrating the teaching of the church Paul had launched. However, at the center of all of this was the worship of Artemis/Diana

- First Timothy 2:9–15 (from braided hair to childbearing) might seem like a garbled knot of random information about women, but to the original readers of Paul's epistle, they were understood to be a unified and *whole* teaching about women

- By saying "let the women learn" in 1 Timothy 2:11, Paul was commanding that the practice of teaching women would be carried out. He *wanted* the women to be taught!

- Rather than meaning that women should adhere to a militant restriction on silence, Paul instead was telling Timothy that women must become "quiet learners" who learn and obey what they're taught about the Gospel before they can become teachers of a material they don't understand

- The Holy Spirit on the Day of Pentecost had already equipped the women in the Upper Room to preach the Gospel to both genders, and Jesus Christ personally inspired them to do the same
- No male or female should teach until he or she has learned

QUESTIONS:

1. FILL-IN-THE-BLANK: In the days before Christ, women were not allowed to learn anything. But on page 134, the author states that by Paul using the phrase "Let the women learn" in 1 Timothy 2:11, he's introducing a "whole new _____ for women."

2. Instead of viewing the phrase "learn in silence" as meaning an "overbearing silence," Donna suggests on page 136 that it probably means a "_____ and _____ spirit from a person who is willing to learn more in an area of life in order to please God."
    A. enthusiastic
    B. cooperative
    C. Both A and B
    D. Neither A nor B

3. FILL-IN-THE-BLANK: She contends on page 137 that the Greek word *hesychia*, describing the type of silence women should carry out when learning, is a _____ kind of silence, not an _____ kind.

4. According to page 138, if women are never _____, then they can never be _____ of correct theology.
    A. present; aware
    B. students; teachers
    C. at home; knowledgeable
    D. None of these are correct

5. SHORT ANSWER: The author states that, rather than the words in 1 Timothy meaning "a peaceful woman preacher/teacher who is preaching the Gospel for the eternal sake of the lost" (page 145),

a more appropriate translation would be that Paul did not allow a woman to do what?

6. TRUE OR FALSE: Donna states (page 147) that the stacked evidence DOES NOT point to 1 Timothy 2:12 as prohibiting women as leaders in the church; rather, it refers to an isolated, cultural/local issue specifically pertaining to the church at Ephesus, wherein woman worshipping Diana would lead people astray spiritually and physically, while also cherry picking parts of *other* religions they liked and incorporating them into their own erroneous interpretations of Christian spirituality.

7. On page 148, Donna relays that _____ _____ are equally vulnerable to false teaching, _____ _____ will be tempted via deception (Eve), and _____ _____ will make bad choices willfully (all the same answer).

    A. both genders

    A. children and adults

    A. prostitutes and usurpers

    A. teachers and priests

8. SHORT ANSWER: According to the author in point number one on page 149, why did Paul say that Adam was first formed, and then Eve?

9. TRUE OR FALSE: According to the author on page 149, when Paul said that women would be saved through giving birth to children, he meant exactly that: In order to make it to heaven, women must have given birth to at least one earthly child.

10. SHORT ANSWER: It's possible that Paul was not addressing all women 1 Timothy 2. According to the author (page 154), what was Paul's number-one priority?

11. FILL-IN-THE-BLANK: On page 155, she says, "If any person does not agree with the words of Jesus Christ, he or she only craves—with an "unhealthy craving"—to _____ _____ _____.

Chapter 5

THE WOMEN JESUS KNEW

CHAPTER 5 SUMMARY:

When Jesus walked the earth, He was revolutionary in His attitude *toward* and treatment *of* women. But before analyzing the women Jesus knew, author Donna Howell takes us through a study of Creation, in an attempt to highlight misunderstandings humans have had about Adam and Eve from the beginning. She then takes us through the Old Testament and reveals how, contrary to popular belief, women have been leaders for thousands of years, including one who was BOTH judge AND prophetess over Israel! We also meet a couple of other women prophets (or "prophetesses"), and the part they played in the life of our Savior.

MAIN POINTS:

- What Adam and Eve saw in the Garden wasn't a talking snake, but a *nachash*—a radiant, divine entity, very likely of serpentine appearance
- Genesis 1:26 says, "And God said, 'Let us make man in our image, after our likeness: and let *them* have dominion" (thus rendering "man" as "mankind" in this Scripture). *Christ Himself* saw that this creation composition was "very good"
- "Fit" and "suitable" are translated from the Hebrew preposition *kenegdo*, which means "equal" and "corresponding to." As such, Genesis 2:18 documents that woman was made to be "an equal person of power and strength, corresponding to Adam"
- Adam was more than likely with Eve when she was tempted in the Garden, which means he is equally as guilty, a "silent accomplice" in the "crime"

- Should either the man or the woman "rule over" the other? Never! To take that approach would be to ignore the "good" Creation God intended and instead embrace the symptoms of a curse that goes against what God wanted from the beginning! At the very least, we must either literally apply *all* symptoms of the curse to our lives today (which means men cannot enjoy their jobs, women in labor cannot take epidurals or relief from childbirth pains, etc.), or we must strive to live the way God intended *before* the curse was pronounced (which means neither men nor women "rule over" the other in God's ideal relationship design), but we cannot apply the "men ruling women" symptom and ignore the other symptoms as the application must remain consistent.

- In Judges chapters 4 and 5, Deborah was the judge *and* prophetess over all of Israel, as chosen by God

- Throughout biblical and world history, there have always been women who have broken the barrier of cultural (and religious) regulation…and fulfilled a destiny role of leadership that changed the course of nations, history, and the Church

- We must never let the archaic and false interpretations of only *two* sections of Scripture (1 Corinthians 14 and 1 Timothy 2) cancel out the hundreds of others that are calling women to action right at this moment

- If we *truly* want the anointing of God on our life, we won't find it by stirring up dirt

- From 2 Kings 22, Huldah was a prophetess, and the fact that her prophecy to King Josiah didn't come true was the result of his disobedience to God, *not* her being a false prophet

- Mary transforms from a scared little girl to a spiritual warrior with a determination that would make Joan of Arc pale in comparison

- Mary was a dauntless, unflinching *fortress* of strength

- From Luke 2:36–38, Anna was a prophetess, and thus, one of the earliest ministers of the Good News—just after the birth of the Savior—was a *woman*

QUESTIONS:

1. SHORT ANSWER: Regarding the "serpent" from Genesis, on page 162, Donna states, "This creature was a being of extreme power and persuasion, most likely a 'professional' accuser within the Divine Council." What was his "major agenda"?

2. FILL-IN-THE-BLANK: According to the author (pages 163), Adam *needed* the power and strength of a woman who would not rule or have dominion _____ him, but _____ him.

3. The author states on page 170 that "the divine order" between man and woman is *mutual* _____.
   - A. admiration
   - B. submission
   - C. cooperation
   - D. respect

4. Judges 5:7 says that Deborah arose as what to Israel?
   - A. Judge
   - B. Prophetess
   - C. Friend
   - D. Mother

5. MATCHING: On pages 177–179, we read of the five issues Deborah addressed as a judge over Israel. Donna then makes parallels to current times. Match the issue Deborah spoke of with the parallel she makes.
   - A. Highways _____
   - B. Decrease in the population of Israel's villages and towns _____
   - C. Israelites were choosing new gods _____
   - D. Wars throughout the land _____
   - E. Praise offering to Yahweh for those leaders who *did* stand up to battle against the condition Israel had found itself in _____
      - I. It seems our radical Christian leaders have all but vanished. Where are our faith warriors?
      - II. Linked to the mass exodus of the Church today

    III. Deborah didn't "arise" like a queen or princess who lives to bedazzle with costly array or exotic dancing, and she didn't "arise" halfway like one who is obedient but stunted by her own lack of confidence. She arose as a *mother*!

    IV. Israelites traded in the Promised Land for "whoring after other gods" (Judges 2:17)

    V. When the Church is vulnerable in its function because of the enemy's grip upon our spiritual welfare, then the enemy "occupies the highways" and causes the people of God to carry out their ministerial calling through the less-efficient side roads

6. On page 181–182, the author states, "The Deborah *we* know, thanks to generations of biased teaching, is one who sat around under a tree and followed the orders of men. The Deborah *Jesus* knew was a _____ _____."

    A. fearless trailblazer

    B. godless heathen

    C. strong leader

    D. mere puppet

7. SHORT ANSWER: On page 183, Donna writes that the "outcome of a prophecy is contingent upon" what?

8. SHORT ANSWER: If Huldah really was a prophetess, why did her prophecy to Josiah, saying he would live and die peacefully, not come true (page 183–184)?

9. On page 186, the author writes that Jesus was raised by Mary, a "very _____ and _____ woman."

    A. strong, silent

    B. quiet, meek

    C. powerful, bold

    D. quiet, humble

10. FILL-IN-THE-BLANK: When Donna talks about Mary, the mother of Jesus, on page 191, she says, "God chose a _____ for a very important role, and He commanded a _____ to support her in that role."

11. SHORT ANSWER: Where does the author state on page 193 that the prophetess Anna likely lived?

Chapter 6

THE WOMEN JESUS SENT

CHAPTER 6 SUMMARY:

In this chapter, author Donna Howell explains why women were considered second-class citizens in the time of Jesus—a cultural belief that continues to this day in some areas of the world. From Old Testament times to Jesus' day, a man could divorce his wife for insignificant reasons (or no real reason at all), and it is this cultural reality that played into the life of the first New Testament revivalist/evangelist, who was a *woman*! Donna also explains that Mary Magdelene was not only more important than you may realize, but also, is probably not who you think she is.

MAIN POINTS:

- In ancient times women were frequently viewed as second-rate citizens. Equality, *within Judeo-Christian context*, was not to be found from any aspect, and this kind of social arrangement influenced the imprinting of the woman's role from thousands of years before Christ and onward
- A Hebrew man could divorce a woman if "she [found] no favour in his eyes" (Deuteronomy 24:1), but a woman *could not* divorce a man; this is an important detail in the story of the woman at the well, whom we have turned into a "loose woman" in our modern cultural teachings, but who truly did not have much choice in who she married or divorced (thus cancelling the idea that she was ashamed for something *she* had done wrong)
- When Christ entered the scene, women were frequently kept indoors and required to remain silent on social or political issues
- The Jewish men *daily* praised God for not making them women!

- Jesus didn't just "allow" women to learn from Him if they happened to be standing around; He specifically sought them out and *went to* them in their court at the Temple (as Scripture identifies) to ensure that they were included in His teaching
- Jesus didn't call a woman to be one of his 12 disciples due to several cultural reasons that would have made such a calling highly inappropriate; that said, there certainly *were* many female disciples apart from the Twelve
- The ministry of Christ, as extended through Paul, was to form a new community of believers that broke tradition: "There is neither Jew nor Greek, there is neither bond nor free, there is neither male nor female: for ye are all one in Christ Jesus" (Galatians 3:28)
- The Samaritans were despised as disgraceful blasphemers
- While we perceive the "five-times divorced woman at the well" to be an "easy woman," someone who sleeps around and has had multiple divorces, it's possible she had been either widowed or divorced by her previous husbands, who did not need her consent to do so
- The Samaritan woman at the well was the first preacher, revivalist, and evangelist of the Messianic Gospel message in human history and as recorded in the entire Bible, and she converted the whole city of Sychar, including the men, to belief in the saving message of God's love. This is an act she accomplished in Christ's very presence, giving Him two full days to run after her, stop her, and alert her that she could not teach the men since that was not a woman's place; instead, however, He remained there and responded positively to the harvest initiated by the woman, which can be viewed as nothing but Christ's endorsement of her as a woman preacher/revivalist/evangelist in His day
- Jewish tradition holds that the woman at the well was baptized on the Day of Pentecost, her name was changed to "Photini," and she went on to be a great preacher and apostle of Christ, repetitiously defying death and leading countless multitudes to God
- Mary Magdalene was known to the semi-early Church (after the tenth century) by the title "Apostle of the Apostles"—a title acknowledging that it was only in recent history that she was stripped of her

title "apostle" and rendered, instead, a tragic prostitute character of the New Testament

- Luke 8:1–3 lists woman who not only travelled with Jesus, but literally *ministered with Him*

QUESTIONS:

1. SHORT ANSWER: According to the author on page 196, how was marriage viewed for centuries among the Hebrews?
1. On page 199, Donna relates a notion from the Talmud that the Jews would have rather _____ their sacred writings than to allow a woman to be taught from them.
    - A. ignored
    - B. hidden
    - C. discarded
    - D. burned
2. SHORT ANSWER: From page 204, what is the stark contrast the author draws between the way the crowd saw the woman caught in adultery, verses how Christ saw her?
3. SHORT ANSWER: What did Donna say would make a woman a disciple in Jesus' time, according to page 204?
4. SHORT ANSWER: In addition to the fact that Jews would never travel through Samaria, what are the three reasons given on page 211 as to why it was so shocking for Jesus to ask the woman at the well for a drink (John 4:5–9)?
5. According to page 215, who was the first person to whom Christ revealed the fact that He was the Messiah?
    - A. John
    - B. Nicodemus
    - C. The woman at the well
    - D. Pontius Pilate
6. TRUE OR FALSE: To this day, in Catholic churches, Mary Magdalene is still known as an "apostle."
7. Page 225 states that women were the first...
    - A. at Jesus' empty tomb

    B. to be told He was risen

    C. to be called to announce this truth to the Apostles

    D. to meet the Risen Christ

    E. All of the above

8. TRUE OR FALSE: On page 227, the author states that she believes Mary Magdalene was the same woman caught in adultery whom Jesus saved by saying the famous line, "He who is without sin, cast the first stone" (Matthew 7:5).

9. SHORT ANSWER: List the reasons on page 228 as to why Jesus' choice to reveal Himself first to Mary Magdalene at the tomb was so culturally significant—then *and* now.

Chapter 7

CREATED HE THEM

CHAPTER 7 SUMMARY:

Author Donna Howell begins this chapter by reminding us that both men *and* women were created by God, in His likeness. Despite what some would have you believe, both sexes have "God-traits" that are unique to them. Donna then gives us a glimpse into her personal life, the "church abuse" she suffered, and how she learned what a "real man" is. She also makes the point that, if we deny ministry and leadership positions to women, we in fact harm the entire Body of Christ, as well as the Great Commission, as we are losing *over half* of our Gospel ministers!

MAIN POINTS:

- When God created humankind, He did so by instilling His image in both genders
- For women, "acting like a girl" is not a weakness (in fact, it can be a great strength and even increase a woman's reach in Kingdom work as this approach is unique from a male)
- When women give up their gentility, their innate femininity, in the quest to "be equal to a man," they are abandoning their God-given image traits in trade for an imitation of those given to the opposite gender
- There are a few classic, no-brainer rules any woman in ministry *must* follow if she is to appropriately handle her potential leadership position
- If you are still single, be sure to talk at length with your potential spouse about what "obedience" and "submission" look like in a marriage and make sure you're comfortable with that relationship *before* you tie the knot!

- If two marriage partners are equally yoked, they will be attached to the same load, and heading the same direction
- Denying women leadership positions within the Church of Jesus Christ harms the whole body
- While it is true that we can ponder about what aborted babies might have achieved in their lives, another valid point is: How many potential soul-winning ministries or churches have been aborted by the rejection of the biblical principles of equality in ministry?
- A minister should be appointed by God based on the qualifications He has bestowed, not based on one's gender, race, or anything else

QUESTIONS:

1. FILL-IN-THE-BLANK: Page 234 relays that "even beyond the scope of ministry, woman has been equal to man in every way since _____."

2. On page 235, Donna says women should "act like a _____; think like a _____."
    - A. lady; baby
    - B. lady; boss
    - C. winner; Christian
    - D. woman; man

3. TRUE OR FALSE: On page 244, the author says that in order to be equal to men, women must sometimes assert themselves aggressively or "act like a man" in order to achieve equality.

4. On page 245 we read, "Leaders of the Church Body, then, have one goal: to _____."
    - A. lead
    - B. pray
    - C. worship
    - D. serve

5. FINISH THE SENTENCE: On page 249 we read that, "the prettier a woman minister is…."

6. On page 252, what two words does the author use to describe what a biblical marriage should look like?

    A. Prayer and balance

    B. Humility and confidence

    C. Submission and fealty

    D. Nurturing and encouragement

7. SHORT ANSWER: Write in one sentence Donna's explanation of a "yoke" when she discusses being "unequally yoked" (2 Corinthians 6:14).

8. SHORT ANSWER: What wonderful "life advice" was given to Donna by a friend (pages 256–257), regarding not being in a hurry to get married?

9. The author relays on page 258 that she "had been overlooking _____ as a crucial factor in a relationship."

    A. love

    B. faith

    C. chocolate

    D. chivalry

10. SHORT ANSWER: List some of the ways the author discusses on pages 260–261 that James, her husband-to-be, earned her trust when they were dating.

11. SHORT ANSWER: What are some of the "rules" Donna has (pages 263–264) by which both her and her husband abide?

12. SHORT ANSWER: Pages 266–267 highlights two examples of when God spoke first to a woman. Who were they?

13. SHORT ANSWER: Finish this sentence from page 270: "If you have an unbelieving husband..."

14. According to research (discussed on page 274), "the average woman" is working _____ hours every week.

    A. 45.5

    A. 60.5

    A. 68.5

    B. 71.5

15. TRUE OR FALSE: Page 277 relates the fact that men and women are created both "the same" and "equal."

Chapter 8

"PREPARE YOURSELF TO MINISTER"

CHAPTER 8 SUMMARY:

In the last chapter of the book, author Donna Howell wraps up this mesmerizing study by challenging women to make themselves ready for ministry. There's something stirring in the air; do you feel it? God is raising up a generation of pastors, evangelists, missionaries, teachers and leaders, both men *and* women. It is imperative we move past our misunderstandings of Paul's references to cultural issues where it regards women in ministry and embrace the fact that *both* genders can be equally effective when being used by God. We will all be met with resistance when moving into a position that helps in building the Kingdom of Heaven, but for the souls of those around us, it is imperative we face these challenges head-on.

MAIN POINTS:

- "Prepare myself to minister"
- The Church is in a state of "falling"—that all-too-familiar sensation that has historically crept over the Body of Christ just before it truly surrenders to sleep as it did in the days leading up to Jonathan Edwards, George Whitefield, James McGready, Dwight Moody, and other mighty and powerful men and women of the Great Awakenings and mass revivals of history
- God's nation is rising
- The Body of Christ is fed through the spiritual food of the Word
- Everyone has an important purpose in the Body of Christ
- The *directive* of God upon one's life doesn't change when that person

is afraid or uncomfortable—he or she *can* choose to disobey God since He has instilled within humanity the gift of free will, but it will not change what God has sent him or her to do!

- If women *do* decide to step into the fullness of their calling, they *will* experience resistance (and this is why it is crucial that we work to establish equality in ministry today for the sake of our daughters and future generations of powerful women of God)
- Whatever your calling is, "whatsoever ye do, do it heartily, as to the Lord"
- Sometimes it is only when ministers press against the resistance around them that they, as a part of the Body, become stronger

QUESTIONS:

1. When Donna felt the winds of change blowing in her spirit, she states on page 283 that there was only one thing to do:
   A. Pray
   B. Cry
   C. Submit
   D. Run

2. FILL-IN-THE-BLANK: Finish this sentence from page 284: "If He so wills a Great Awakening to change the world from this day forward, then it only takes _____."

3. SHORT ANSWER: On pages 283–285, the author says that, for years, she wanted to be "the appendix" in the Body of Christ. What did she mean by that?

4. Where does Donna say that "the sharks gathered" (page 292)?
   A. Family
   B. Work
   C. School
   D. The Church

5. FILL-IN-THE-BLANK (from page 292): "So when the winds of change stirred me and I felt the Holy Spirit telling me I was not—as I had hoped—going to get by with existing 'out of sight, out of mind,' the _____that fell upon me was great."

6. SHORT ANSWER: Name the two serious issues the author says we all have to deal with (page 297).

7. SHORT ANSWER: On page 299, what does the author mean when she says, regarding following the Will of God, that she is still in her season of "do-it-afraid-ing"?

8. On page 300, what word does Donna say is synonymous with "minister"?

    A. Servant

    B. Leader

    C. Man

    D. Christian

9. TRUE OR FALSE: On page 302, the author states that just because someone is a follower of Christ and has the Holy Spirit in his or her heart, doesn't necessarily mean they are called as a minister (servant) of God.

10. SHORT ANSWER: According to page 302, what can women who stand behind the pulpit expect?

ANSWER KEYS

Chapter 1 Answer Key

1. starving, encouragement
2. **C**; She is a woman
3. Because, according to the author: "If this plan or this undertaking is of man, it will fail; but if it is of God, you will not be able to overthrow them."
4. **True**
5. No, Donna states, "I am not a feminist, I don't participate in women's lib movements, and I don't think men are 'the enemy.' I love my husband and obey him consistently. I submit to him. I am ardently grateful for male ministers and the essential role they have played, still play, and will continue to play in the Church. By no means do I intend to 'liberate women from male oppression' or any such nonsense."
6. **False**; "berating" responses often come from those who are *not* in leadership.
7. Donna says radical "feminism teaches that in order for a woman to be equal to a man, she must believe men are beneath her and spread the word that men are less intelligent than she is, that she is the superior sex, and that a chief goal among most men is to reduce women to little more than slaves. The only way to achieve true equality, feminism imparts, is for women to act like men and tower above them in the process."
8. extreme injustice, subsequent entrapment
9. "(S)kewed interpretation can—and has—been the road upon which scores of false teachers, preachers, and prophets have led millions of people into misunderstanding."
10. said, application
11. competent knowledge, culture

12. Donna relays that we need to "comprehend the process of getting information out of an ancient culture and making it relevant to our modern lives."

13. "(B)ecause that means letting go of all they've known or believed up to that point, so they hold on to what's familiar, what's comfortable, always referring to the others in their support group for confirmation of a path that is biblically incorrect."

14. **C**: Both A & B

15. **True**

Chapter 2 Answer Key

1. Examples of answers: Can women even speak in church? Can they sing, or preach, and if so, for how long? If she is allowed to speak, during what part of the service? Can she receive ministerial license, or be labeled a "prophet"?

2. **E**: All of the above

3. fortuneteller, vocal instructor

4. **True**

5. **B**: corrected

6. **D**: Priscilla was more "active" as a teacher and leader in their home church

7. **False**: The English translation Paul used was phrase, "fellow worker," and the Greek translation of *synergos* is "a companion in work."

8. **True**

9. Euodia and Syntyche

10. **D**: All of the above. The word *Prostatis* is derived from the prefix *pro*, "before," and the verb *istemi*, "to stand"—i.e., to stand before others or over others (similar to "overseer") with the authority that a patron would have held at that time.

11. Embraced

12. **False**

13. Discuss: As Donna summarizes: "The fact that the epistle to the Galatians was written as a response to a *salvation* issue and not to Church leadership positions is not proof that Galatians 3:28 is

irrelevant to that subject. It's another chink in the distracting-competition-within-the-Body-armor. It merely speaks of Paul's innate nature. If anything, it further supports his willingness to see equality in Church leadership, because it's yet another verse that serves to tear the social walls down and embrace a full oneness as a team: the objective being the Great Commission, the tools being Body members who do not squabble against each other about church politics and legalism while thousands around us are dying daily. Was the verse written to address women as preachers, teachers, and prophets? No, and it would be improper exegetic practice to claim that it was. Does the verse support the *whole* message of Paul throughout the *whole* of the same author's epistles as it stood for widespread and far-reaching equality among believers who are 'neither Jew nor Greek, neither bond nor free, neither male nor female' in the work that the Holy Spirit poured out upon everyone equally? Does the verse support the idea that, within the realms of this very endeavor, we are 'all one in Christ Jesus'? If a person is willing to see the verse as the heartbeat of the man named Paul, then he or she will 'hear' the 'voice' of the man who constantly cried out for equality, and he or she will know that this verse in Galatians is yet another extension of the man who saw us all 'as one' in Christ's *work*."

Chapter 3 (Part One) Answer Key

1. Absolute; relative; normative
2. Witnessed and condoned the stoning of Stephen, arrested, imprisoned and persecuted believers, received permission to take his attack to Damascus
3. Prosperous commercial center for sea trade, capital city of Achaia, central seat of Roman government, protected by mountains, worship of the pagan goddess Aphrodite was common, had many festivals, population between 100,000 and 600,000, one thousand cult prostitutes at the temple of Aphrodite.
4. "Corinthian girl"
5. **True**

6. **D**: Their loyalties were divided
7. **A**: Divided
8. **E**: All of the above
9. **C**: Sexual immorality; dissension
10. charity; love for others who may or may not agree with what we believe
11. **False**; NO CHRISTIAN TEACHER OR LEADER, whether male or female, should act in this way

Chapter 3 (Part two) Answer Key

1. "…blatantly associate herself with the behaviors of temple prostitutes and common pagan practices"
2. **True**
3. Because the second that power plays are introduced, it becomes mankind's game.
4. **B**: Following these verses in 1 Corinthians 14 we find the infamous passage about women keeping silent in churches.
5. talk, talking
6. Specifically to Corinth, thanks to the *hetairai* and *pornai* prostitutes who had already formed an entire cultural acceptance of women who shared "enlightened" opinions and beliefs regarding spirituality and theology, the Christian women in Corinth would have been especially chatty in their newfound freedom. The *hetairai* and *pornai* had "controlled the city" so to speak, and paved the way for women to enter any building under any circumstances and assert themselves with questions, tongues, and other less-than-ideal utterances. Whether the Christians in this church were prostitutes, Jewish converts, Gentile converts, travelers, or simply curious women wandering in from the street (and there is historical evidence to suggest a mixture of these, since Corinth was such a beehive of commercial trading), they would have walked into a building with confident, well-educated, vocal woman seeking theological answers.
7. **D**: restrictions
8. **C**: Pagan outbursts

9. Because this would change the meaning of the verses "women keep silent" to giving a quote concerning common thinking of men at the time (as in, "*you* say 'let your women keep silence in the churches'"). If this is true, we not only have evidence that Paul praised women leaders in the early Church, we also have evidence that Paul rebuked any man who would attempt to silence a woman.

Chapter 4 (Part One) Answer Key

1. Goddess of fertility, considered the Great Mother of Asia, all life began through her, that Adam was created through Eve's rib—not the other way around—and that salvation came through *gnosis* (enlightenment) of pagan entities, goddess of the hunt (through archery), wilderness, forests, hills, animals, childbearing, virginity, and the moon. It was believed that she could both bring and relieve disease in women; she could control animals with her blessing; she was able to create all life without the need for a male's involvement (a kind of "virginal birth" idea); and she served to protect little girls.

2. **False**; Surprisingly, due in part to the widespread, societal veneration of a goddess in Ephesus, women were given many privileges and freedoms that are not typical of the treatment toward women in most ancient cultures. There were certainly restrictions (for instance, a woman could not vote), but as it was believed that a woman's body during (quite perverted) religious rituals assisted men in determining the will of the gods, women were naturally given much license to weigh in on religious topics.

3. sexual worship

4. Demetrius—a wealthy silversmith who made silver idols of Artemis/Diana—instigated a near riot when he perceived his idol-making trade was vulnerable under the increase of Christianity

5. They believed Artemis/Diana, their primary deity, created life without a male's participation, which on the surface, seemed similar to the story of Jesus having been created and brought into the world with no help from a man.

6. **False**; They practiced "syncretism" (a blending of religions). They

felt like they could "cherry pick" what they liked about Christianity and embed it into their current religious practices and beliefs.

7. His concern was with a woman attending church in modesty and humility, and in making sure that her appearance in a place of worship would be for the right reasons (to worship, not to attract the attention of surrounding men).

8. **B**: Prostitutes

9. **False**; Applying the "cultural issue" argument in one verse and the "absolute regulation for all times" argument in the very next verse in sequence *when the context for both verses is the same from one to the next* is an outright misapplication of Scripture

10. **D**: Priscilla and Aquila

11. cultural

12. order

Chapter 4 (Part Two) Answer Key

1. freedom

2. **C**: Both A and B

3. harmonious; oppressive

4. **B**: students, teachers

5. Carry out "an imposition of the subject's will" while someone's "self-interest is being overridden."

6. **True**

7. **A**: both genders

8. He was reminding false teachers in Ephesus that even if Artemis/Diana existed in the minds of her believers, according to the Holy Scriptures that Christianity was built upon, Eve was NOT formed first in the Creation order—and these false-teacher women would be wise to accept that they, like Eve, were not given an authority advantage in the Creation order just because their goddess religion told them so. In any case, *this verse was never about who could teach and who couldn't* (as the context makes abundantly clear), but about correcting the paganized Eve-came-first theology that Ephesian women had brought into the church.

9. **False**; Jesus, our Savior, was NOT "created by" Eve (or Artemis/ Diana) without help from a male, as the cult in Ephesus claimed, and Paul was correcting this. All life on Earth involved the male seed of Adam to produce the eventual Mary (mother of Christ), through whose womb the Savior would be born, and this is the true meaning behind Paul's string of words about women being saved through childbearing. His statements therefore have nothing to do with a woman's salvation being dependent upon having babies.

10. Weeding out the false teaching, since at least one female was (and perhaps many were) at the forefront of the "spiritual pollution."

11. bicker over words

Chapter 5 Answer Key

1. To reverse the beauty of what God had created
2. over; with
3. **B**: submission
4. **D**: Mother
5. Answers:
    A. Highways: V. When the Church is vulnerable in its function because of the enemy's grip upon our spiritual welfare, then the enemy "occupies the highways" and causes the people of God to carry out their ministerial calling through the less-efficient side roads
    B. Decrease in the population of Israel's villages and towns: II. Linked to the mass exodus of the Church today
    C. Israelites were choosing new gods: IV. Israelites traded in the Promised Land for "whoring after other gods" (Judges 2:17)
    D. Wars throughout the land: I. It seems our radical Christian leaders have all but vanished. Where are our faith warriors?
 E. Praise offering to Yahweh for those leaders who *did* stand up to battle against the condition Israel had found itself in: III. Deborah didn't "arise" like a queen or princess who lives to bedazzle with costly array or exotic dancing, and she didn't "arise" halfway like one who is obedient but stunted by her own lack of confidence. She arose as a *mother*!

6. **A:** fearless trailblazer
7. "...the God-fearing response of its recipient."
8. The first word of God, as given through the mouth of Huldah, said he would live and die peacefully. The second word of God, as given through the Lord's servant Necho, said he would be destroyed if he stood in Necho's way, which he did. Thus, God allowed Josiah to be killed in battle at a young age.
9. **C:** powerful; bold
10. Woman; man
11. The Temple

Chapter 6 Answer Key

1. As a business contract, the woman being property of the man: an object to own, not a person to be loved or valued.
2. **D:** burned
3. *They*—the crowd—saw a harlot. A dog. A "pitcher of filth" whose blood on the temple floor would have hardly been worth cleaning up after. Christ saw a *person*. He took *her* side over the leaders of the "Church" of that day.
4. Women were present while Christ taught
5. First, Christ was a Jew, so He was not supposed to speak to a Samaritan. Second, Christ was a Jewish *man*, so He really wasn't supposed to speak to a woman. Third, Samaritans were "unclean," so accepting a drink of water from a Samaritan would have certainly, by tradition of the Jews, made Him ceremoniously "unclean" as well.
6. **C:** The woman at the well
7. **True**
8. **E:** All of the above
9. False; It is cultural tradition (due in part to the infamous twenty-third homily delivered by Pope Gregory the Great in 1591), *not the Word of God*, that has confused the patroness Mary Magdalene with these other characters, eventually and erroneously rendering Mary Magdalene a prostitute.
10. Women in Christ's day were not recognized as legitimate witnesses.

So, when Christ appeared to Mary Magdalene, making her the first person to see and experience His resurrected presence, He was directly challenging this cultural norm. He did not choose to appear to a man, nor did He tell the women to track down a man for Him. He simply told the *women* to go and tell the *men*. He trusted the message of His resurrection, the foundation of the Gospel, to a woman first. And though some would correctly assert that Jesus did not personally commission Mary Magdalene in this moment to become a pastor, teacher, preacher, or any other office so often held by men—and therefore, suggesting He "turned Mary into a preacher" at this point in the narrative would be applying too much liberty from the Greek—this moment still infers much in regard to what women are allowed to do in the eyes of the Savior! *Jesus Christ, in this moment, reversed and dispelled forever the notion that a woman can't be trusted with His message, and that she can't deliver it to a man.* That is absolutely relevant!

Chapter 7 Answer Key

1. Creation
2. **B**: lady; boss
3. **False**; We should celebrate how we are *different* from men (thereby expanding the pool of voices reaching lost souls who will respond to various outreach attempts differently), rather than make it our aim to prove how we can be the same as men. The historical battle to achieve "sameness" has skewed God's original design, instigating a ceaseless, and fruitless, battle of the sexes…and ironically, proving "sameness" almost always increases to proving "betterness" of one over the other.
4. **D**: serve
5. "…the more finger-pointing sharks will have to talk about if she slips in her wardrobe choices even once." (This may not be fair, but it *is* true…at least in our current day, and until women are considered by other people to be fully equal in Kingdom work, women making the bold decision to hold positions of leadership MUST be very careful to do so modestly!)

6. **A**: Prayer and balance
7. A yoke is a wooden bar that joins two oxen and supports the weight of the load they pull.
8. "Know who you really are and what you really want before you promise your life to someone."
9. **D**: chivalry
10. He respected her, treated her like a gem, cared more about her mind than her mascara—and above all, he truly cared about her happiness and God-given calling upon her life.
11. Neither goes anywhere alone with a member of the opposite sex; neither spends an unusually large sum of money without checking with the other; neither commits to host an event at their house without checking with the other; neither obligates the other to attend a social function without checking with the other. In short, both Donna and her husband, James, thoroughly *respect* the money, time, space, relationship, and overall life that they share together, in order to accomplish the work God has called them both to carry out in ministry together. As such, "submission" or "winning an argument" remains a nonissue.
12. Samson's mother, and Mary, mother of Jesus.
13. "…try as hard as possible to see him in the same way God saw you before you surrendered your life to Christ."
14. **D**: 71.5
15. **False**; We are *not* the same, but we *are* equal.

Chapter 8 Answer Key

1. **C**: Submit
2. one
3. She wanted to sit in the back of a building somewhere and be silent for a living. Nobody needed to know she was ever there except her boss. She wanted to be unseen and unheard.
4. **D**: The Church
5. discomfort
6. fear and discomfort

7. She's saying that everyone feels fear, but we should follow God's voice, His will, even while we're afraid. If you're uncomfortable, then follow the will of God uncomfortable. If you're afraid, do it afraid, but just *do it*.

8. **A**: Servant

9. **False**; Any true follower of Christ who has the Holy Spirit in his or her heart has already been called as a minister (servant) of God, according to these verses in Romans and 2 Timothy. It does not mean that every true follower of Christ has to fulfill the role of a preacher.

10. Resistance

REFLECTION QUESTIONS

Chapter One Reflection Question

Chapter 1 opens with the author's very successful appearance on *The Jim Bakker Show* (including not one but *two* standing ovations!), soon followed by the vile comments on the recap video by YouTube viewers. On a scale of 1–10, how bad would these terrible comments hurt you? Be honest.

Chapter Two Reflection Question

What has been your experiences with women in leadership positions? In our modern day and age, do you feel women still have to fight men as hard as they did 50 years ago to be respected?

Chapter Three (Part One) Reflection Question

Discuss a passage of Scripture you misunderstood, either by your own doing or someone else's, for a long period of time, and the process by which you discovered the true meaning.

_____

_____

_____

_____

_____

_____

_____

_____

_____

_____

_____

Chapter Three (Part Two) Reflection Question

Discuss the women in leadership positions from whom you found great inspiration at any point in your life.

_____

_____

_____

_____

_____

_____

_____

_____

_____

_____

_____

Chapter Four (Part One) Reflection Question

In Ephesus we find that, while they worshipped a female goddess and women were revered in certain aspects, they were still not considered equal to men in social rights and privileges. Give your opinion on how different our modern society is (if you think it's different at all).

_____

_____

_____

_____

_____

_____

_____

_____

Chapter Four (Part Two) Reflection Question

At what point does a "theology discussion" become "bickering over words"? Why do you think it seems men are more likely than women for this to turn into an argument?

_____

_____

_____

_____

_____

_____

_____

_____

_____

_____

Chapter Five Reflection Question

Discuss women you have either personally known or studied who broke down cultural and/or religious barriers. Was their work for the Kingdom ultimately helpful? Were there areas these women could have improved in the work they carried out?

Chapter Six Reflection Question

Talk about a time you were made to feel like a second-rate citizen, and how you worked through it (if indeed you *have* worked through it). How does this experience relate to potentially fulfilling a leadership role in ministry?

Chapter Seven Reflection Question

With feminism and advancements in thinking regarding women in the 20th and 21st centuries, do you agree with the author's "classic, no-brainer rules any woman in ministry *must* follow" on pages 246–252? Why or why not? In *your own* area of the world or culture, what might you add to, or tweak from, this list to ensure the Christians in your region might more effectively embrace and maintain women in leadership roles?

Chapter Eight Reflection Question

When in your life have you had to face the uncomfortable season(s) of "do-it-afraid-ing"? What did you learn through this experience? (Both positive learning and negative learning are permissible answers; answers do not need to be restricted to ministerial duty.) How might you draw inspiration from this experience to encourage other women who are facing similar self-assurance challenges? And finally, after reading through the whole book and taking this class, are *you, personally* prepared to enter into the fullness of God's ministry calling on your life with newfound boldness and determination? Please share with the rest of the study group what that calling may look like and how you plan to commit to a new level of reaching the lost.

Made in United States
Orlando, FL
09 December 2024

55241000R00038